Standing Together

Standing Together
The Story of Natan Sharansky

Leah Sokol

Green Bean Books

Green Bean Books

First published in 2024 by Green Bean Books,
c/o Pen & Sword Books Ltd,
George House, Units 12 & 13, Beevor Street
Off Pontefract Road, Barnsley
South Yorkshire S71 1HN

www.greenbeanbooks.com

© Leah Sokol 2024

All rights reserved. No part of this publication may be reproduced, stored in or introduced into a retrieval system, or transmitted, in any form, or by any means (electronic, mechanical, photocopying, recording or otherwise) without the prior written permission of the publisher. Any person who does any unauthorized act in relation to this publication may be liable to criminal prosecution and civil claims for damages.

PJ Our Way edition: 978-1-80500-097-6
Green Bean Books edition: 978-1-80500-057-0

Library of Congress Cataloging-in Publication Data available

Typeset in Garamond 12/16pt
by JCS Publishing Services Ltd, www.jcs-publishing.co.uk
Printed and bound by in Great Britain by CPI Group (UK) Ltd,
Croydon, CR0 4YY

Chapter One

Natan Sharansky was five years old when he first learned the rule: Never say what you really think.

Natan was a quiet, happy boy. He lived in the Soviet Union with his parents and his older brother, Leonid.

Like all brothers, Natan and Leonid sometimes fought with each other. Natan was stubborn; if he thought he was right, he would stand in the corner without moving, refusing to apologize. But their family was full of love, kindness, and humor, and everything always worked out.

One day in 1953, Natan's kindergarten teacher told the class that she had bad news.

"Today there will be no laughing and no playing," the teacher said. "Our beloved leader, Comrade Stalin, is dead. School will be closed for several days so we can all mourn."

No school! Natan did his best not to smile.

Joseph Stalin had been the leader of the Soviet Union for over twenty-five years. Every morning, Natan and

Standing Together

the other children in his class chanted: "Thank you, Comrade Stalin, for our happy childhood."

And now he was dead. How could the nation go on?

Sad music filled the streets. Huge pictures of Stalin hung everywhere.

But earlier that day, Natan's family had sat down together. His father had looked around carefully before he spoke. They shared their apartment with several other families, and he needed to be sure no one else could hear him.

"There is something you should know," Natan's father said. "Comrade Stalin was not a great leader. He killed many innocent people, and he told everyone to hate the Jews. We're better off with him dead."

The boys stared at him.

"But," he added, "*don't tell anyone* what we really think. You must act the same as everyone else."

He spoke in a low voice. In the Soviet Union, all aspects of people's lives were controlled by the government. The Soviet secret police, the KGB, paid millions of people to eavesdrop on their friends and neighbors and report what they said. The KGB wanted to make sure that no one criticized the government. People who expressed the wrong opinions or discussed the wrong topics would be taken by the KGB. Everyone knew people who had disappeared into the KGB's prisons.

Natan's home was filled with trust and warmth. His parents talked to their children as openly as they could, and their children listened to them and valued their advice. They knew they couldn't talk freely with anyone else.

That day in kindergarten, the children sang songs honoring Stalin, and many of them cried. Natan sang along with the rest. He looked around, wondering which of the children were truly sad and which were just pretending.

There was no way to know.

Natan (far left) with his brother Leonid and their parents. (Sharansky Family Archive)

Standing Together

Natan—then called Anatoly—lived in Ukraine, which was one of the republics of the Soviet Union. His family lived in two rooms in an apartment that housed several other families. Seventeen people shared one kitchen and one toilet. Every day, people spent hours waiting in line—not just for the toilet, but at the stores too. There were lines for everything they needed—milk, eggs, soap. If you didn't get in line fast enough, there wouldn't be any supplies when your turn came.

The Soviet Union was based on a political system called Communism. Under Communism, all property was owned and managed by the government instead of by individual people. It was believed that this would make all people equal, and no one would be poor. But under the leadership of Stalin, Communism led to severe food shortages. Millions of people died of starvation, especially in Ukraine. Millions of others were jailed or killed to preserve Stalin's power.

After Stalin's death, people became less afraid, and there was more they could talk about. For the first time, Natan's father took out a picture of himself with his three brothers. Natan was surprised. Until then, he had thought his father only had two brothers.

He now learned that his father's oldest brother lived in Israel. He had moved there many years ago, and Natan's father had never dared mention him until now.

Standing Together

Growing up, Natan knew that he was a Jew. It was on his parents' identity papers. On the fifth line, under nationality, it said *Yevrei*, which meant Jew.

Natan grew up hearing grown-ups talk constantly about "the fifth line problem." Many schools and jobs would not accept Jews at all. Others would take only a few Jews.

His brother Leonid had been told by one school not to be excited that he had done well in his exams. "I won't let Jews into *my* school," the interviewer sneered at him.

People joked that the reason most of the synagogues were closed was because they couldn't find any non-Jewish rabbis, but of course no one would hire a Jewish one! Of course they knew the real reason the synagogues were closed was because the Soviet government did not want anyone to practice religion. The government did its best to stamp out any knowledge of Jewish religion or culture among the millions of Jews in the Soviet Union.

That meant the only thing Natan knew about being Jewish was that it made your life difficult. All the children knew that being born a Jew was the worst thing that could happen to you. His classmates often teased and bullied him. They said Jews were cunning, greedy, and cowards. Even some of his friends would say, "You're such a good guy. It's a pity you're a Jew."

Standing Together

His father often told him that being Jewish was nothing to be ashamed of. "But be careful," he added. "Don't talk about it too much."

All in all, being Jewish seemed like something it would be great to escape from.

~

Natan knew exactly where he wanted to escape to: the world of math and science.

In other subjects, like history or literature, people had to be careful. The government told them how to teach history and which books were allowed. Often, the state would change its mind about what people should believe, which could be dangerous for the people studying those subjects.

As a child, Natan saw this happen often. Every couple of years, his father would receive a letter telling him that the government had changed its mind about someone, and the entry about that person in the encyclopedia had to be removed. Natan watched his father cut out the pages about the person he was no longer supposed to read about, and glue in new pages that the government approved of.

But even the Soviet government couldn't change the rules of the universe, so scientists could study those subjects without worrying about the state.

Standing Together

Luckily, Natan loved anything related to math and puzzles, like logic games and Sherlock Holmes stories. He especially enjoyed chess, which his mother had taught him. He would sit in the park where the adults played chess, waiting for someone to be left without a partner. When that happened, the lone adult would sometimes agree to play chess with a child, since there was nothing else to do.

That adult would be in for a surprise when the seven-year-old won the game!

Natan playing chess in 1961, at the age of thirteen. (Sharansky Family Archive)

*Here's Natan at his high school graduation.
(Sharansky Family Archive)*

Even so, Natan knew that getting into a good science school wouldn't be easy—not with that fifth line on his identity card. He would have to do better than everyone else. In high school, he studied extra hard for test after test, getting perfect scores. He participated in the right Communist youth activities. He sang the songs the government approved of.

It all seemed worth it when he got into one of the top science schools in the Soviet Union. In the "castle of science," as he thought of it, he could focus on studying the mysteries of life.

The fact that he was Jewish, he hoped, would no longer matter. Not to other scientists, and certainly not to him.

Chapter Two

Natan loved his school, and when he grew up he loved his job. He worked on developing programs to teach computers to play chess.

Scientists were free of many of the restrictions that other Soviet citizens faced. The Soviet Union and the United States were engaged in what was called a "Cold War," where they did not directly fight each other, but competed in other ways. Each country wanted to be the strongest power in the world. Because of this, the Soviet Union urgently wanted to develop better weapons than the United States. That meant that scientific advancement was important to them, and they made sure scientists were treated well.

For the most part, scientists in the Soviet Union didn't care about politics. After all, they were studying the laws of science and math—laws that would never change. Temporary things like rights, freedom, and justice were obviously not as important.

Standing Together

Natan thought of himself as a good Soviet citizen and did his best to behave just like everyone else.

In 1967, when Natan was nineteen, news came over the radio: the Egyptian army was about to attack Israel. All the surrounding Arab countries were going to join Egypt's attack. Soviet radio predicted an immediate victory for Egypt and the complete destruction of Israel. There would no longer be a Jewish state.

Natan had believed he didn't care about being Jewish. He never really thought about Israel, which had been founded only two months after he was born. But suddenly, he found that he cared very much about a war happening over a thousand miles away.

He wasn't the only one. Soviet Jews gathered around radios, listening to reports of Israel suffering one defeat after another.

But several days later, the truth became known.

In this conflict—known as the Six Day War—Israel was victorious. They destroyed Egypt's air force, which consisted mostly of Soviet planes, in a single morning. They went on to push back all the Arab armies and even conquered new territory.

Israel's victory was so overwhelming that the Soviet government couldn't pretend it hadn't happened.

The Jewish state, which was supposed to be weak and defenseless, had beaten the allies of the Soviet Union. Suddenly, the anti-Semitic jokes changed. Jews were no longer made fun of for being greedy cowards; now they were attacked for being dangerous bullies.

Soviet Jews didn't know whether to be proud or afraid. But they were now aware that they had a history, a people, and a country—and many of them wanted to know more about it.

Secretly, they started copying books about Israel and Judaism, passing them around from one person to another.

The more Natan read and studied, the more he felt that "this was the history, these were the people, that was the country I wanted to belong to."

Three years later, Natan had his first run-in with the KGB—the secret police force that everyone was afraid of.

What had Natan done to earn their attention?

He had translated an article from English to Russian and put it on the bulletin board in his dorm building.

The article was about Andrei Sakharov, one of the top scientists in the Soviet Union. He had shocked everyone when he wrote an essay in which he dared to point out the problems in Soviet society. Sakharov was fired from his job for writing the essay, and no paper in the Soviet Union would publish it. But it was copied secretly and passed from one person to another.

After Natan translated the article, the KGB wanted to talk to him.

"What is your connection to Sakharov?" a KGB agent demanded. "What literature did he send you? Where are you giving it out?"

"I never met Sakharov," Natan protested. "I'm a loyal Soviet citizen, just like you."

At the time, he thought he was telling the truth. He had gotten used to forcing himself to believe what he was supposed to believe. He no longer even noticed that he was doing it.

This was his first interview with the KGB ... but it would not be his last.

In 1973, at the age of twenty-five, Natan made the hardest decision of his life. He asked to leave the Soviet Union and move to Israel.

This was not a simple thing to do. People in the Soviet Union were not allowed to leave the country without permission. Asking for permission—by applying for an "exit visa"—was dangerous. Everyone would despise you for being a traitor. You would probably lose your job and most of your friends. Your neighbors would be told that you wanted to leave. The KGB would become suspicious of you and start looking for an excuse to arrest you.

And after all that, you probably would not even be allowed to go. Most Jews who wanted to move to Israel were refused permission.

⁓

The first step in applying for an exit visa was to get a letter from your job. When Natan did that, a public meeting was arranged so the people he worked with could criticize him for abandoning the Soviet Union. Hundreds of people came to the meeting. The head of the group started the discussion with this introduction: "Does anyone have a question for Sharansky, who betrayed us all?"

People had plenty of questions!

"How can you leave the Soviet Union and go to our enemies?"

"Israel made war to conquer Arab land! How can you help them?"

"In Stalin's time, they would have known what to do with people like you!"

What people did not expect was for Natan to start answering the questions!

Standing Together

"How am I a traitor? It is perfectly legal to apply to leave."

"Israel responded to an attempt to destroy it. Any country has that right."

For the first time, Natan was publicly saying what he believed. He felt like he had spent his whole life carrying a giant weight, and had gotten so used to it that he had stopped noticing it. Now, at last, he was able to think what he wanted to think—and to say what he thought.

No matter what happened next, he felt that he was finally free.

Chapter Three

For a long time, Natan did not get an answer to his request for an exit visa. He spent his time learning more about Judaism and Israel and studying Hebrew.

One day he was hanging out with some friends when a tall, quiet young woman came up to them, shivering in the snow. Her name was Natasha, and she told them that she was worried about her brother, who had joined a Jewish demonstration a week ago. She hadn't seen him since.

Natan explained to Natasha—who would later change her name to Avital—that he knew the routine for demonstrations: her brother would be in jail for two weeks and then he would be released.

Natan and Avital liked each other at once. Because Avital was shy and pretty, many people thought she was delicate. But Natan could see, from their very first meeting, that her quietness hid an enormous strength. Avital thought that Natan looked like a free person—

something that was very rare in the Soviet Union, and that she knew, from her own experience, required great effort. But to Natan, it seemed to come naturally.

Avital had grown up in a town in Siberia, a cold, harsh territory in the east of Russia where people were often sent as punishment. Her parents were dedicated Communists who worked for the government and believed everything they were supposed to believe. They had not even told Avital she was Jewish until late in her childhood; the fifth line on *her* identity card said "Russian."

When Avital was twenty years old, she read a secret copy of a speech given by another woman—a Jewish woman not much older than herself, who had tried to escape the Soviet Union, failed, and been put in prison. Part of her speech was in Hebrew, a language Avital had never heard of. She was so intrigued that she took the risk of meeting a man who knew Hebrew and could translate it. When she first saw this man, he was praying, and his face seemed lit up by a warm light.

Avital wanted to feel that light within herself. She felt that she was being stifled in a dark, cold world, and she was determined to break out of it. She and her brother now lived together, and the two of them desperately wanted to get to Israel.

"Are you studying Hebrew?" Natan asked Avital when they met.

"Yes," Avital said.

"Maybe you could study in my group," Natan suggested. "I know about a thousand words."

"Me, too!" Avital said.

It wasn't true; she knew much fewer than that. But she wanted to study in the same group as Natan so she could get to know him better.

It worked!

Studying Hebrew wasn't technically illegal, but the KGB did their best to stop it. They followed people, arrested them, and took away any Hebrew or Jewish books they found.

Soviet Jews asked tourists to smuggle in Jewish and Hebrew books from Israel. Sometimes the books were stuffed into suitcases and buried in a forest, with instructions passed secretly about where they were so people could dig them up. People made copies of these books by taking photographs of each page and then developing the photographs privately.

These kinds of books were called *samizdat*—illegal publications that people copied on their own and passed around secretly. A popular explanation of *samizdat* was: I write it all by myself, I publish it all by myself, I distribute it all by myself, and I sit in jail for it all by myself.

Standing Together

For many Jews, studying Hebrew from these books was the first step in learning more about Israel and Judaism.

Natan and Avital were soon invited to their first Passover seder—a ceremonial meal during which Jews discuss their ancestors' escape from Egypt thousands of years ago. As they talked about the ancient Jews' journey to the land of Israel, they occasionally glanced out the window at the black cars in the streets below, where KGB agents were keeping track of the people at the seder.

Natan quickly realized that Avital knew much less Hebrew than she had claimed. By then it didn't matter. Natan and Avital were deeply in love. They knew that they belonged together and that they wanted to spend their lives in Israel.

The government had other plans. Soon after meeting Avital, Natan was told that his exit visa had been refused. He would not be allowed to leave the Soviet Union.

Natan was not the only Jew who was refused permission to leave. There were many Jews who had given up their jobs and their place in society in order to ask for an exit visa but were now trapped in the Soviet Union forever. Those people were called "refuseniks"—the ones who were refused.

Standing Together

Natan joined other Jewish refuseniks who were doing their best to pressure the Soviet Union to let them leave.

Sometimes they protested. They made signs saying "Give us visas to Israel!" and "Let my people go!" and ten or fifteen people would gather together and hold up the signs. Usually they managed to wave their signs for only a minute or two before the police swooped in, pulled down the signs, and arrested them all.

In secret conversations with tourists, they discovered that Jews in other parts of the world were also protesting for the refuseniks—and protests were legal in those countries! So the refuseniks focused on creating petitions and reports about Jews who wanted to leave the Soviet Union. Jewish tourists would smuggle the reports out of the country—sometimes by hiding them in their underwear—and send them to Jews in the rest of the world.

They all worked together to let the world know what was happening to Jews in the Soviet Union. Natan, who spoke English better than most Russians, was often in charge of talking to journalists.

During this time, he changed his name. Until now his name had been "Anatoly," but now he wanted to be called Natan. Natan was his great-grandfather's name, and the name his grandfather had wanted him to have. But his parents had been afraid to use it because it sounded too Jewish. His grandfather still used to call him "Natanchik," though.

Standing Together

Before long, everywhere he went, Natan was followed by the KGB. Sometimes they arrested him and brought him in to yell at him and threaten him. Most of the time they just followed him, trying to make him afraid.

Natan overcame his fear of the KGB agents by making fun of them. Once he called KGB headquarters indignantly: "I have a complaint about the agent following me today. He's so drunk he's not doing a good job." Another time, two KGB agents were so anxious not to lose track of Natan that they jumped into a taxi with him. Natan turned to them and said, "You can share my taxi, but only if you pay half the fare!"

They did!

One day Natan was grabbed off the street and thrown into jail for two weeks. He was one of many. President Richard Nixon of the United States was coming to the Soviet Union, and the government wanted to make sure no one caused trouble during his visit.

While Natan was in jail, Avital got some news: her exit visa had been approved. She was free to leave for Israel. But if she didn't leave within two weeks, she couldn't go at all. She decided that she would use the visa and leave, and hope that Natan would be able to join her in Israel soon. Before she left, she wanted to marry Natan.

Standing Together

Natan and Avital had already tried to get married. The government refused to give them a marriage license. But this time Avital managed to find a rabbi who knew Natan and agreed to perform the wedding even without the government's permission. Avital and the rabbi worked feverishly to prepare for the wedding while Natan was in jail with no idea that this was happening.

Avital in June 1974. This picture was taken by Natan's father a few days before Natan and Avital got married. (Sharansky Family Archive)

*Natan, aged twenty-six, in the same year.
(Sharansky Family Archive)*

Avital didn't know for sure that Natan would be released from prison in time for their wedding, but she prayed that he would. On the morning of the wedding, she still hadn't heard anything from him. She left the house anyway and went to invite all her friends to her wedding that evening.

Her prayers were answered. Natan came home and they were able to get married. It was the first Jewish wedding either of them had ever seen, and it was their own. They danced, singing songs in Hebrew, until late in the night.

The next morning, Natan and Avital went to the airport. It was very hard for them to part from each other.

"See you soon in Jerusalem," Natan told her. "I'll be there within six months at the latest!"

But they both knew it would probably be a lot longer than that.

Chapter Four

The six months stretched into a year, and then into two years. With the help of tourists, Natan and Avital managed to exchange letters, and sometimes they even found ways to talk on the phone. But they missed each other very much.

In Israel, Avital was reunited with her brother, who had been granted a visa and moved to Israel a little while before. She lived with some friends while she worked on improving her Hebrew.

As she walked the sunny, open streets of Israel that she had dreamed of for so long, she often imagined that Natan was with her. "He would look so natural in that crowd," she thought. "No one would even guess that he was a new immigrant!"

Standing Together

In the Soviet Union, Natan continued working with the refuseniks day and night, often without time to prepare proper meals or get enough sleep. Natan was known as "the spokesman," helping the refuseniks communicate with the outside world. KGB agents still followed him everywhere; they sat in their cars outside his apartment all night. Yet he felt more free than he ever had before.

Natan also began helping his hero, Andrei Sakharov,

Natan (left) started working with Andrei Sakharov in 1975. Here he is with Andrei (centre) and Yelena Bonner (right). (Courtesy of Connie Smuckler and Enid Wurtman)

the scientist whose essay had caused Natan's first encounter with the KGB. Sakharov had started a human rights group to publicize how the Soviets were persecuting their own people—both Jews and non-Jews. Sakharov was not Jewish, and his goal was to change the Soviet Union from the inside. But he also supported the refuseniks' goal of leaving the Soviet Union for Israel.

Some people thought it was strange that Natan was part of both groups. The refuseniks wanted to focus on getting Jews out of the Soviet Union, and were afraid that the Soviets, who were angry about the human rights group, would take revenge on the Jews. The human rights people thought that what mattered was rights for everyone, and that Natan should not focus so much on Jews who wanted to leave for Israel.

But to Natan, the two went together. They were part of the same struggle. Being Jewish was what gave him the freedom and strength to help others ... and the more free he became, the more Jewish he felt.

One thing was for sure: the KGB saw both movements as a threat to the Soviet Union. The government wrote articles in the Soviet newspapers accusing the refuseniks of being traitors and "gangsters." Then an article appeared claiming that Natan was a spy for the United States.

Everyone knew that someday soon, the KGB would put Natan in prison. He packed a "prison bag," with some warm clothes and a book, and carried it everywhere he went.

Standing Together

But for some time, nothing happened. There were now eight KGB agents following Natan. Everywhere he went, they made a tight circle around him. When he wanted to greet someone, he had to stick his hand out through a mass of agents. But none of them made a move to grab him.

"You know," a friend told him, "the longer this goes on, the more I think you might not get arrested after all."

"I think so, too," Natan said. "It's almost a pity. I'm so well prepared."

Then one day, Natan left his weekly Hebrew lesson and was grabbed by six men. They pushed him into a car and drove him to a KGB prison. It happened so fast that he didn't even have his prison bag with him.

"You are accused of treason," he was told, "and of spying for the United States. If you are found guilty, you will be shot."

Even though he had known this was coming, Natan felt shocked and very alone. He had to put his hands between his knees so the KGB agents wouldn't see that he was shaking.

"Admit that you are guilty," they said, "and we'll go easy on you. You won't have to worry about being killed. We'll send you out of the country instead, just like you wanted. You can join your wife. All you have to do is confess."

But they made a mistake when they mentioned, *your wife*. Natan thought of Avital in Israel. He knew that as soon as she heard of his arrest, she would start working to help him.

Suddenly he didn't feel alone. To the KGB agents' shock, he smiled.

"I am innocent," he said. "There is nothing more to discuss."

⸻

Natan was placed in a cold, narrow cell. He was allowed one hour outside for exercise, and the rest of his time was spent in the cell or being questioned by the KGB.

The KGB agents were excellent at getting prisoners to confess to things they were not guilty of. They used many tactics to make prisoners feel completely alone. They talked to Natan for hours. They yelled questions at him, threatened him, and told him that all his friends had already said he was guilty.

But Natan did not feel alone. He felt that he was part of the Jewish people. He believed that his friends would stand by him. And he knew he would always be connected to Avital.

He treated his sessions with the KGB like a chess

game. He wrote out his moves in advance on the toilet paper the prisoners were given. He memorized the moves, then flushed the toilet paper. While the KGB agents were asking him questions, he was trying to get *them* to reveal what was happening in the world outside his prison. He gathered clues from what they said and then pretended he knew more than he really did. He made confident statements about what he guessed was happening, then watched their reactions.

He confused the agents by joking with them.

"Your case is very serious," a KGB agent thundered. "We have eleven agents handling it."

"Oh, good!" Natan said. "I'm glad to hear there's no danger of unemployment in this country."

Another time, he asked the agents, "Did you hear what happened? Brezhnev [the Soviet leader] was really upset that the Americans landed a man on the moon. So he called in his scientists and said, 'We are going to beat the Americans! We're going to land men on the sun!'

"'But that's impossible,' the scientists said. 'They'll be burned to a crisp!'

"'Don't worry,' Brezhnev assured them, 'I've thought of everything. We'll send them at night.'"

Natan could see that the agents wanted to laugh. But of course, they didn't dare. Instead they yelled at him, pounding on the table: "How dare you insult our glorious leader?"

Natan smiled. "Look," he said. "You can't even laugh at a joke you think is funny. Are you so sure that I'm the one who's in prison, and you're the ones who are free?"

He made up a short prayer using the Hebrew words he knew, asking God to give him the strength to leave prison and reach the land of Israel without betraying himself. Every time he was led to talk to the KGB he recited the prayer twice. It was the only part of his daily routine he could control.

Sometimes the KGB put him in a "punishment cell." This was a small, damp, freezing cold cell where prisoners were given barely any food. It was impossible to get warm and impossible to sleep. They put Natan in the punishment cell for days, taking him out only to ask him questions.

But every day, Natan reminded himself: My goal is to live as a free person, and that goal depends only on me.

After almost a year, it was time for his trial.

Natan knew that it wasn't going to be a real trial. When the government brought political charges against a person, that person was *always* found guilty. Not once in Soviet history had any political prisoner been released.

But the Soviets wanted it to look like a real trial. So they gave him a chance to read the "evidence" against him. They had gathered loads of evidence. There were fifty-one files, many of which consisted of over three hundred pages.

Natan was thrilled. Here was more information than he had been able to get in the past eleven months! For one hundred days, from morning to evening, all he did was read the evidence. He didn't really care what it said about him—he knew he had no chance of being freed. He wanted to find out what was happening in the world outside the prison. Had the KGB succeeded in turning his friends against him and crushing the refusenik movement, as the agents had claimed?

As he read the reports, it became obvious: the opposite was true. Not one of his friends had agreed to help the KGB.

One of the pieces of evidence was a film that had been made about him in England. Natan insisted on seeing it. And there, on the screen, was Avital! She was leading a demonstration in London, demanding that he be freed.

Natan barely noticed the rest of the film. He was too busy looking for glimpses of Avital. There she was again, speaking in perfect Hebrew!

"I need to see this film again," Natan said. "My Hebrew and English aren't good enough for me to understand everything the first time."

He watched the film again and again until the KGB

officer in charge began to yell at him. He warned Natan not to think that demonstrations could save him. "What do you think, that your fate is in the hands of those people and not ours?" he shouted. "They're nothing more than students and housewives!"

The film was taken away. There was no more evidence to review. Natan's trial was about to start.

Chapter Five

Avital had discovered that she could not start her life in Israel without Natan. She learned Hebrew and enrolled in art school, but she was constantly waiting for Natan to come ... always hoping and always afraid for him. She was determined to help him get out of the Soviet Union.

But once she saw the article accusing him of being a spy, she knew the Soviet government was planning to arrest him.

"I wanted to run out into the street and to scream," she said. "But I couldn't move."

A knock on the door brought her back to life; friends of hers had come for their weekly Torah study sessions. When she explained what had happened, her friends took her to visit the head of their yeshiva (school of Jewish learning). The rabbi of the yeshiva, who was old and very sick, was lying down in bed. But after listening to Avital, he pulled himself up to a sitting position. He decreed that his yeshiva should be closed for a few days so that all the students and teachers could concentrate on trying to help Natan. They worked frantically to get the news of his upcoming arrest into the press, and tried desperately to contact Natan.

The chief rabbi of Israel sent a message all around the world, saying that Jews everywhere should pray for Soviet Jews.

All Avital could think was that she had to speak to Natan. She had to tell him that she would be with him forever, no matter what happened. But it was impossible. His phones, and the phones of all his friends, had been disconnected.

Despite this, Soviet Jews managed to get a letter out, telling people that the Soviet Union was trying to crush the refusenik movement. There were beatings and arrests. All Soviet Jews were at risk.

"They will not force us to turn back in our struggle," the refuseniks wrote. "We are proud of our past and present. Am Yisrael chai! [The nation of Israel lives!]"

Avital decided to travel to other countries to ask for help. She didn't have a passport, which normally took at least a month to get. But everyone wanted to help her. She received her passport in fifteen minutes.

While Natan was in prison waiting for his trial, Avital traveled around the world, talking about him. She spent all her time on trains and planes, in meetings and at demonstrations, explaining what was happening to her husband and to other Soviet Jews.

Standing Together

One person after another asked her the same question: "How can we help?"

Some Jews had been trying to help Soviet Jews for a long time. And the KGB were right: a lot of them were students and housewives.

There was the Student Struggle for Soviet Jewry, an organization started by groups of college students in New York City. Even before Natan's arrest, they had been arranging rallies and demonstrations, shouting: "Let my people go!"

There was a group of women who called themselves the Thirty-Fives. The group had been started by thirty-five women in England, who had all been about thirty-five years old when they started demonstrating for a thirty-five-year-old Soviet Jewish woman who had been put in prison. The Thirty-Fives slept in the streets to draw attention to the freezing conditions in Soviet jails and attended the Russian ballet wearing prisoners' uniforms. The attention they got put pressure on the Soviet government to make changes in their prisons. By now, the Thirty-Fives consisted of thousands of people all around the world.

Jewish songwriters wrote songs about Soviet Jews. Rabbis left a seat empty in their synagogues to represent Soviet Jews who were not free to go to synagogue. Thousands of ordinary people risked their lives to travel to the Soviet Union as "tourists" so they could secretly take books to the refuseniks and smuggle their letters and protests out.

Many of these people already knew who Natan was. He was the reason a lot of them knew about the plight of Soviet Jews and had decided that they had to fight for them. Now Avital made him the center of their movement.

There were demonstrations all over the world. Hundreds of petitions were sent to Soviet representatives. Fourteen New York rabbis chained themselves to the fence in front of the Soviet headquarters at the United Nations. President Jimmy Carter of the United States declared on television that the accusations against Natan were a lie, and he was not a spy.

For Avital, it was all a blur. She barely had time to eat or sleep. The telephone never stopped ringing and the news crews never stopped coming. She spoke in schools and in synagogues. She met rabbis and leaders, senators and movie stars.

The Soviets started attacking her in the news. They said she wasn't really Natan's wife. They said *she* was a spy. At one point they said she didn't actually exist!

Avital knew how huge and powerful the Soviet Union was. Sometimes, she realized just how futile her battle was, and how little hope she and Natan had.

Then she thought about Natan. In her mind, she heard the songs they had sung at their wedding. She heard the crowds supporting him, shouting, "Am

Standing Together

Yisrael chai!" All around her, she saw the nation of Israel, protesting and demonstrating and working to free their fellow Jews on the other side of the world.

And she knew she would never give up.

Natan could not defend himself; it was up to her. She would make sure people remembered him. She wouldn't let him disappear.

Natan refused the government-appointed lawyer and instead defended himself at his trial. He had no trouble proving that the charges against him were false. He was allowed to question some of the witnesses, and it was easy to show that they were lying.

One witness claimed that he had seen Natan meeting with Americans and reading over a treaty that the Soviet Union opposed. Natan showed that at the time when the meeting supposedly happened, those Americans had not even been in the Soviet Union.

One of the witnesses was a supposed janitor who claimed he had found, in the garbage of a newspaper office, a report in English about Natan. The janitor said the report made him suspicious, so he turned it in to the KGB. Natan asked the janitor to read a different article in English. The janitor couldn't, because he didn't know how to read English.

Standing Together

Another witness said he had seen Natan secretly meeting with an American congressman. Natan showed that the witness had obviously never seen the congressman, because he didn't even know the congressman was Black!

Natan knew that none of this mattered to the court. They had already decided their verdict, and in the end it would be as if the trial had never happened.

But his brother, Leonid, was allowed into the courtroom. Natan was really talking to him—and through him, to the world.

Leonid had until now been a regular Soviet citizen, with a family and a job and no interest in moving to Israel. Even so, he stood behind his brother completely. When the KGB took away the notebook he had brought to court, he wrote notes on the palm of his hand.

Natan told his brother that despite everything that had happened, he did not regret applying to leave for Israel. The last five years, he said, had been the best of his life. He felt part of the Jewish people and part of their history.

"For two thousand years," he said, "the Jewish people had seemingly no hope of returning to Israel. But every year they said to each other, 'Next year in Jerusalem!' And that is what I say today to my wife and my people. Next year in Jerusalem!"

"And to the court," he finished, "I have nothing to say."

Standing Together

Natan stared at his brother. They smiled at each other as the judges found Natan guilty and read his sentence: thirteen years in jail.

"The whole world is with you!" Leonid cried as they led Natan from the courtroom.

The trial was over.

Chapter Six

Natan's last words to the court, before he was led away to prison, were, "I have nothing to say."

He meant it.

Natan decided that he would no longer talk to the KGB. Now that his trial was over, he didn't want information from them. All they could give him were privileges that would make his life physically easier. And those, he decided, were not worth it.

The KGB weren't going to give up so easily. They could not stand to see a single person defy the Soviet system.

"We've broken better men than you," they told him.

The KGB controlled everything in the prisoners' lives: how much food they ate, how much fresh air they breathed, how often they got to see sunlight. A basic belief of Communism was that people's physical needs mattered more than anything spiritual. The KGB believed they could use those physical needs to get prisoners to talk to them and agree to work with them.

But Natan would have nothing to do with them.

He knew refusing to talk to the KGB would make his life in prison much harder. But he also knew that it was the only way that, even in prison, he could remain free.

༄

Two weeks after he was put into a new prison, the guard who delivered Natan's daily soup passed him a message along with it. "Read it in private," he whispered, and moved on.

That was how Natan discovered that he was not the only refusenik in this prison. The message was from one of his heroes. Natan had organized demonstrations to try to get this man free, and now they were in prison together.

Natan and the other refuseniks were kept separate and not allowed to communicate with each other. But they found ways, especially because many of the regular prisoners respected and helped the "political" prisoners—the ones who were risking everything, not for money, but for their beliefs.

Sometimes a message could be left in the exercise yard for another criminal, who, back in his cell, would lower the message by a thread from window to window until it got to the person it was meant for. Sometimes they taped messages to the wall, written in Morse code. Sometimes they scratched messages into pieces of soap in the shower room where every prisoner went once a week.

The most effective way to talk was through what they called the "toilet telephone." Since the cells were connected by the plumbing system, Natan would take a floor rag, dip it in the toilet, and wring out the water. He would do this again and again until the toilet was empty, and the prisoner in the next cell would do the same. Then, by sticking their heads into the toilet, they could talk to each other through the pipes.

They spoke in Hebrew. That made it harder for the KGB to listen in, and it also helped Natan continue his Hebrew lessons even inside prison. Every time he finished a conversation, Natan wrote down the new words he had learned, then started practicing for the next conversation.

These methods took a long time and were very dangerous. They had to make sure no guards caught them talking to each other.

Luckily, Natan trusted his cellmate, a Catholic from Lithuania who was in prison for creating a human rights group. (Lithuania, like Ukraine, was one of the republics of the Soviet Union.) The KGB had probably put them together to make things harder for Natan, because at

Standing Together

first his cellmate was prejudiced against Jews. But over time, Natan and his cellmate grew to like each other very much. Each of them believed in something bigger than himself, something that mattered more than what the KGB could do to them. Even though they believed in different things, they knew they could trust each other.

Even so, Natan got caught sometimes. When he was, he was sentenced to the punishment cell.

Luckily, Natan already had methods for surviving the punishment cell. He sang, thought about the past, and solved chess problems in his head. The first time he was sent to the punishment cell, the KGB thought they had a chance to get him to talk. The head of the prison came to visit him and told him he had better behave, or he would be kept in the punishment cell even longer.

"What's wrong with the punishment cell?" Natan said. "Someday I'll go to Israel, and people will ask me about the punishment cell. I have to be able to tell them what it was like."

"That's exactly why you're in prison!" the head of the prison said. "Because you want to say bad things about the Soviet Union."

"What bad things?" Natan demanded. "Are you saying the conditions in the Soviet prisons are bad?"

That was the end of that conversation.

Standing Together

Life in prison was physically difficult. Sometimes, Natan's "exercise hour" was so early in the morning that it was still dark, and he went months without ever seeing sunlight. There was barely any food, and the food they did get was disgusting. On most days, the soup had dead flies in it. One criminal submitted a complaint to the prison, saying he wanted his flies served separately.

Before long, it became obvious to Natan that he would not be in Jerusalem next year, or perhaps for many years after that.

He knew that Avital was still fighting for him. Even though he was not given most of the letters sent to him—and those that he did get had many lines blacked out—he was able to figure out that there were people demanding that he be freed.

He also knew that the Soviet Union, which couldn't provide all the food its people needed, wanted to trade with the United States. Because the movement for Soviet Jews was so loud and powerful, the Soviet Union sometimes had to let prisoners go in return for the trade agreements they wanted.

When one of his fellow refuseniks disappeared from jail, Natan met with the head of the prison just long enough to trick him into admitting that his friend had been set free.

It gave Natan hope, but he knew that hope was another way the KGB broke prisoners. There were some prisoners who spent all their time trying to figure out if they might be released soon. If a jailer smiled at them, they thought it was because they were about to be set free. If the soup was worse than usual, they despaired that they would be in prison for ever. They could not control their emotions, which made it easy for the KGB to control them.

I must not become like that, Natan thought. *I have to accept that I might be in jail for the next thirteen years—or maybe even for my entire life.*

Natan never stopped thinking "Next year in Jerusalem." But it was no longer his hope. Instead, it was his reason for why he was in prison, and why he must never give in to the KGB.

Chapter Seven

Leonid had told the truth at the trial. The world *was* with Natan. The speech he made at his trial was printed in newspapers everywhere. To many, Natan represented all Soviet Jews.

And Avital was determined to keep it that way.

Avital hated being in the spotlight. Her greatest wish was for a quiet life. "All I want," she told a friend, "is to be at home, mending Natan's socks and changing our babies' diapers."

Instead she flew all around the world. She gave speeches, organized demonstrations, and raised money. Despite her shyness, she had no hesitation in demanding the release of her husband from anyone and everyone.

She would sneak into press rooms at important meetings and talk about Natan, even when it made the United States government angry at her.

During a historic meeting between Israel and Egypt, she walked right past the security guards and up to the

Avital in 1980, during a trip to Amsterdam to raise awareness about Natan. (Nationaal Archief)

president of the United States, the president of Egypt, and the prime minister of Israel. "What about my husband's case?" she asked.

Once, when she accidentally called a British politician in the middle of the night, he shouted at her, "Do you think the whole world revolves around you and your husband?"

"Yes," Avital said. "In fact the whole world does revolve around this. There are Jews in the Soviet Union who are being held in prison simply for their desire to be Jewish. Maybe your role in history, right now, is to help end this tragedy."

Her humility and sincerity affected everyone she met. And Avital was smart as well as determined. She knew how to inspire people. She knew how to get the attention of newspapers. She knew that the way to pressure the Soviet Union was to pressure the United States government.

And she was counting on Jews all over the world to help.

Every time Soviet leaders tried to meet with American leaders—there the demonstrators would be, holding up signs with pictures of Natan and other refuseniks, singing, "Am Yisrael chai!" and "Let my people go!"

Businessmen, politicians, students, rabbis, teachers—they all came together and made their message heard: We will not forget about our Soviet brothers and sisters.

Standing Together

We will fight for them loudly and publicly. And we will never give up.

∽

After three years in prison, Natan was transferred to a "labor camp," where he was supposed to serve the rest of his sentence. Even though the labor camp involved forced work, it was much better than prison. Natan could breathe fresh air and get his possessions back.

One of his possessions was a small Psalms—a book of prayers and songs from the Hebrew Bible—with a black cover. A few days before his arrest, a tourist had given the Psalms to Natan, explaining that Avital had sent it. Natan wasn't allowed to keep it with him in prison because it was printed outside the Soviet Union. But during his transport from one prison to another, Natan had managed to tear out the front page of the book where it said it was published in Tel Aviv. Then he started asking for it back, pretending that it was not a religious book but a "collection of folk songs" and that it had been published in the Soviet Union.

Not every prison guard knew that there was no Jewish literature published in the Soviet Union. And of course, none of them could read Hebrew. So eventually, Natan got the book back, and he began reading Psalms every day. Even though his Hebrew wasn't good enough to understand every word, he felt that the spirit of the Psalms lifted him up from the world of the prison and made him feel closer to God. He especially loved the verses in Psalm 23:

Though I walk through the valley of the shadow of death,
I will fear no evil,
For You are with me...

The precious book of Psalms that Avital managed to get to Natan. (Sharansky Family Archive)

Standing Together

"You," to Natan, meant everything that helped him remain free in his mind: Avital, Israel, God. As long as he felt connected to something bigger than himself, he truly did not fear the evil of the KGB.

He continued to refuse to talk to them. The KGB reacted by finding reasons to put him into a punishment cell. They also took away his book of Psalms, claiming that it was a "harmful influence." (To the Communist government, anything religious was considered harmful.)

Natan was determined to get the book back. He refused to do any more work until it was returned to him.

He was immediately thrown back into the punishment cell. This time, he was kept there for almost two hundred days. He became so weak that eventually they had to take him out to put him in the hospital.

But at least they finally gave him back his Psalms.

Soon after that, though, the KGB decided that they would no longer allow him to write letters to Avital or to his family.

Natan knew what the KGB was doing: they were trying to break his connection to his family, his wife, and his people. He could not let that happen.

He had only one weapon left, the most desperate weapon a prisoner could use: a hunger strike. He would refuse to eat until they let him write to his family again.

The Soviet government could not have prisoners dying of starvation in their prisons; the news of that would get out and make them look bad to the rest of the world. But a hunger strike would only help Natan if people outside the Soviet Union knew about it. So he made a plan to get the word out.

He got himself thrown into the punishment cell (again). The punishment cell was right below the cell of a friend of his. That person, also a dissident, had previously sent Natan messages by arranging to work in the camp kitchen and sticking notes inside Natan's potatoes. Since then, the two had arranged a way to communicate by tapping messages in Morse code on the radiators. Through this method, Natan let his friend know that he was going to start a hunger strike in three months.

His friend was released, and Natan had to hope he had gotten the message out. He started his hunger strike on the day he had planned. That day, he knew from his mother's letters, was Yom Kippur. That meant that as he started his fast, millions of Jews would be fasting with him. As always, what kept Natan going was the knowledge that he was not a single person standing alone against the KGB. He was part of the Jewish people, part of their history, part of their struggle.

And they were part of his.

Chapter Eight

News about Natan's hunger strike reached the United States. The reports said that he was very ill and weak. It seemed more and more likely that he would die in prison.

American Jews had been demonstrating for Soviet Jews for decades now. One demonstration had followed another, and still the Soviet government hadn't budged. Journalists weren't interested anymore. They wanted to hear something new.

"Did he die?" one reporter asked Avital. If he had, that would be something worth writing about.

Still, Avital had reason to hope. The new president of the United States, President Ronald Reagan, invited Avital and other dissidents to come visit him in the White House. Avital stepped out of line, grabbed his hand, and wouldn't let go. "I have to speak to you," she said.

The picture of President Reagan looking kindly at Avital appeared on the front pages of major newspapers.

Standing Together

It sent a clear message to the Soviets: the president is on our side.

Finally, the Soviet government gave in. They said that Natan was terribly weak and ill because of his hunger strike. If Natan wrote a letter asking to be released early for medical reasons, the Soviet government would let him go.

The American diplomats were very excited when they told Avital the great news. They didn't understand why her expression didn't change.

"He won't do it," she said, and turned and walked away.

The diplomats stared after her, confused and frustrated. They thought she was crazy.

The hunger strike made Natan weak and sick. Every few days, the authorities force-fed him to make sure he didn't die of starvation. He spent most of his time half-conscious, dreaming of his wife and of Israel.

Finally, after one hundred and ten days, the authorities relented and he was allowed to send letters.

The prison doctor warned him that the hunger strike had damaged his heart. "You have to be careful," he said.

But soon they stopped letting him write letters again, and Natan began another hunger strike.

Finally, the prison authorities gave in. Not only did

they let him write letters, but they allowed his mother and brother to visit him. His mother was horrified by how thin and unhealthy he looked.

Natan's brother explained to him that the Soviet government wanted to make an agreement with the Americans, but because the American public cared so much about Natan, the United States would not go ahead while he was still in prison. So the Soviet government had agreed that if Natan signed a statement asking them to release him early because of his health, they would grant that request and Natan would be free.

Natan had now been in prison for six years.

"We think you should do it," Leonid said. "And I heard from Sakharov that he thinks this would be acceptable."

"What about Avital?" Natan interrupted. "Does she want me to do this?"

"No," Leonid said. "She does not ask you to do anything."

Natan sighed with relief. He already knew what his answer was going to be.

All these years, he had held onto his one goal, the only thing that was in his control: to remain free. He could not go back to a life where he said what the KGB wanted him to say.

"I will not sign this document," he said. "It would be admitting that I deserve to be here, and that they are

Standing Together

releasing me because they are merciful. But I am innocent, and they are unjust."

Natan's brother and mother were not surprised, even though his mother was very disappointed.

The meeting ended. For the first time, the guards did not stop Natan from hugging and kissing his mother. But when he went to hug his brother, they angrily grabbed his arms.

"That's already too much!" they said, and took him back to his cell.

Soon after Natan refused the KGB's offer, conditions in prison became worse. The authorities made the punishment cell even harsher and put people in it more often. Worst of all, the Soviet government passed a new law saying that they could increase prisoners' sentences without a new trial.

Natan wasn't surprised. After all, the whole reason he was in prison was because the government didn't like his opinions. Why would they release him when those opinions hadn't changed?

Natan also discovered that his victory over the mail was only temporary. The authorities allowed his mail for a while ... and then they took it away again. Natan declared another hunger strike. Eventually, they gave in, and he got his mail back. Then after a while, the mail stopped, and he was forced to engage in yet another hunger strike.

Often he dreamed that he was on a plane, flying west. The plane landed and he saw Avital. He ran toward her ... and then the cold woke him, and he opened his eyes in the darkness of the punishment cell.

Chapter Nine

Natan had now been in prison for nine years. During those years, three Soviet leaders had died and been replaced. All had been pressured to release Natan, and nothing had changed.

Instead, for most of the time that Natan had been in prison, the Soviet government had worked even harder to suppress all Jewish activity inside the Soviet Union. More people were being arrested and no one was allowed to leave. When Soviet Jews managed to get news out to the West, it was all bad: the refusenik movement was being crushed.

People in the rest of the world were losing energy and hope. It became difficult for Avital to raise enough money to continue the struggle. At one point, she was reduced to standing in the lobby of an Israeli hotel and asking tourists for money.

Still she refused to give up. Just as she had on her wedding day, she worked without stopping so that she

Standing Together

and Natan could be together, even though she had no idea when she might see him again.

She knew that she was really fighting for the sake of all Soviet Jews. This feeling, along with the support of her friends and her faith in God, gave her the strength to go on.

"Tomorrow might be the day he is freed," Avital insisted. "Tomorrow we will start our family."

But by now, nobody except her believed that she would ever see Natan again.

⸻

The new leader of the Soviet Union—the fourth since Natan's arrest—was Mikhail Gorbachev. He, like the others, did not seem interested in doing anything about Soviet Jews.

But he did want to make treaties with the United States. The Soviets needed to trade with the United States to help their economy. They were also worried about new weapons the United States might be developing, and they wanted both countries to agree to restrict the kinds of weapons they would create.

Most people in the United States wanted this as well. When President Reagan of the United States agreed to meet with Gorbachev in Switzerland, there was great hope that the two leaders could create a better relationship between the United States and the Soviet Union. Maybe there would finally be peace between the two superpowers.

But American Jews were not going to let the world ignore the subject of Soviet Jews.

During the meeting between Reagan and Gorbachev, there were demonstrations and newspaper articles and petitions. Activists were warned not to try to disrupt the meeting in any way. Nevertheless, several people—including one of Natan's old prison-mates—went up to the Soviet airline office near the meeting and said they wanted to purchase a flight to Israel for Natan. When they were refused, they sat down, put pictures of refuseniks on the wall, and began studying Torah loudly. They were arrested and placed in prison for two days.

Avital was also there, with a letter for Gorbachev's wife. In the letter, she asked the other woman to help her see her husband again. "I send this letter to you," she wrote, "a wife and mother, because I am being deprived of my right to be a wife and mother." She stood for hours in the snow in front of the Soviet mission, wearing a prison uniform and holding the letter.

"You can keep saying Sharansky is a spy," President Reagan said to a Soviet representative, "but my people trust that woman. As long as you keep her husband and other political prisoners locked up, the United States will not be able to trust you."

Standing Together

Thousands of miles away, in a labor camp deep in the mountains, Natan was suddenly yanked out of the punishment cell and taken to the hospital. There, he was served massive amounts of food. He was even given eggs, which he hadn't eaten in so long that he had almost forgotten what they tasted like. He was injected with vitamins and allowed to walk outside for two hours a day. He gained more than twenty pounds in four weeks.

He didn't know the reason for all these changes. Obviously, the prison authorities didn't want someone from outside the prison to see what terrible condition he was in. But who was it? Were they going to allow him to meet his mother and brother again? Did they just want him to meet with some higher-ups in the KGB, to make him yet another offer that he would have to refuse?

Or … were they going to release him?

He knew better than to hope. And yet he couldn't help hoping.

He was in the hospital for a month. Then a group of KGB agents took him to a car and shoved him inside, just as they had that day nine years ago when he was first arrested. He was driven to another prison and put there.

Days passed in the new prison, and Natan sank into despair. Despite himself, he had been hoping for a miracle.

Then the KGB came for him again. They made him change out of his prison uniform into regular clothes. Even with his additional twenty pounds, the clothes were too big for his underweight body. He had to hold his pants up with a drawstring.

"Leave everything behind," they told him, and took away his book of Psalms.

Natan immediately threw himself down in the snow. To his surprise, the guards quickly gave him back the Psalms.

He was put on a plane—just him and the guards. From the position of the sun, he could see that they were flying west. To freedom? Could it really be true?

"You are being expelled from the Soviet Union," a KGB agent said to him, and at last Natan was able to believe it: he was free.

He clutched his little black Psalms book in his hands. Years ago, he had chosen the Psalm he would read when he was released. He recited it now: "You have brought me up from the grave. You have kept me alive."

The plane landed in East Germany, which was then a Communist country controlled by the Soviet Union. "Get out of this plane," the KGB agent told him, "and walk straight to that car over there, which will take you to the border [with democratic West Germany]. Agreed?"

"Agreed?" Natan said. "You know I don't make agreements with the KGB."

Standing Together

So he walked in a zigzag all the way from the airplane to the car.

After a short drive, he got out of the car to walk across the border—a four-inch line that had been cleared of snow.

Natan jumped with joy as he crossed that line. The drawstring around his waist tore, and as he entered the free world, he caught his pants just before they fell down.

∽

Avital was waiting for him at the airport in West Germany.

They stared at each other. Natan was still painfully thin, wearing too-big pants and a large Russian fur hat. Avital was wearing a long skirt and had a kerchief covering her hair.

Natan ran toward her. They hugged each other and cried. The last time they had seen each other had been twelve years ago, at a different airport, when Natan had told her they would see each other in six months.

"Sorry," Natan said. "I'm a little late."

∽

Standing Together

Natan and Avital finally reunited after twelve years apart. (HERNIK NATI GPO)

Natan held Avital's hand tightly to convince himself that he wasn't dreaming. A part of him felt like if he let go of her, he would wake up back in the punishment cell.

He was flown to Israel and greeted by joyous, excited crowds. The entire government of Israel was waiting to meet him. Everyone wanted to hug him and shake his hand. Avital stood by his side, laughing and crying at the same time, while Natan thanked everyone for all they had done to save him.

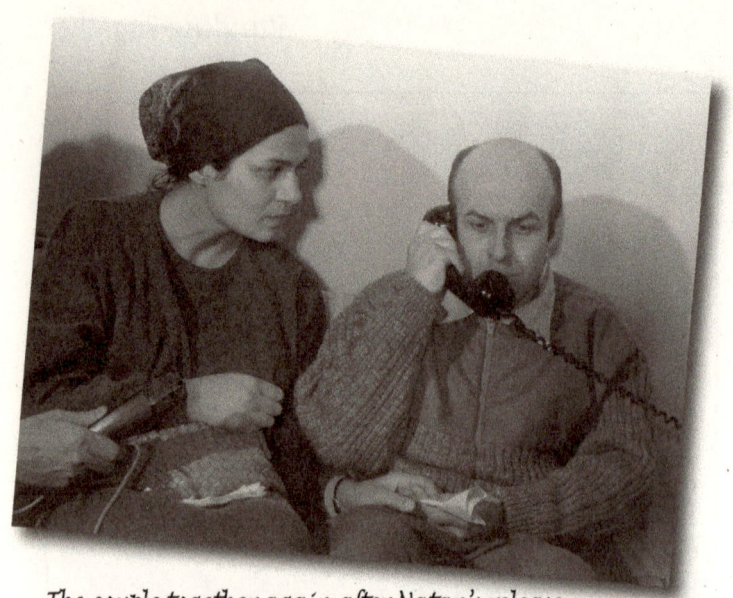

The couple together again after Natan's release on February 11, 1986. (Government Photographic Office, Israel)

As he stepped off the plane in Israel, Natan was welcomed by Israeli Prime Minister Shimon Peres. (GPO)

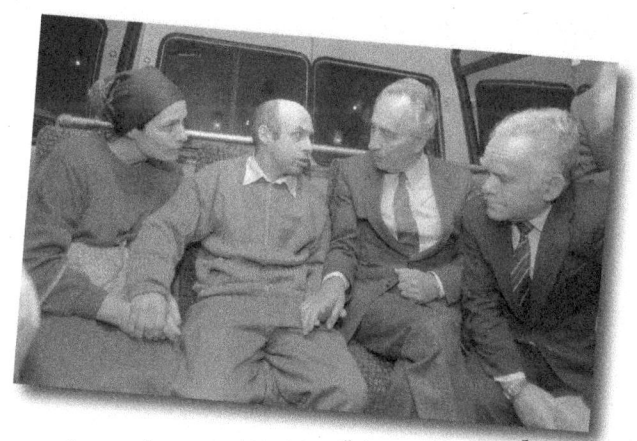

Natan with Avital, Prime Minister Shimon Peres and Deputy Prime Minister Yitzhak Shamir just after he landed in Israel. (Government Photographic Office, Israel)

Natan and Avital also met Israeli minister Ariel Sharon when they arrived. (Government Photographic Office, Israel)

Standing Together

Everyone was amazed by how calm he was. But it was easy for him to be calm, because he had run out of the ability to be surprised. That morning he had woken up in prison, and here he was in Israel getting a phone call from President Reagan.

"If they had told me that the next phone call was going to come from King David," he said later, "that would have made just as much sense to me."

Evening found him at the Western Wall in Jerusalem, surrounded by a crowd of singing, dancing people. Finally, he let go of Avital's hand. People carried him on their shoulders to the Western Wall. With his Psalms book in his hand, he kissed the Wall and said the blessing he had long planned for this moment: "Blessed be He who frees the imprisoned."

Avital had been to the Wall many times over the past twelve years, praying for Natan's freedom. Now, at last, Natan was here. They were together and in Israel.

"It was just one long day," she told him later that night. "I arrived in Israel in the morning. You arrived in the evening. It was just one very, very long day in between."

Surrounded by crowds of people, Natan went to the Western Wall on the day he arrived in Israel. "Blessed be He who frees the imprisoned," he said.
(SAAR YAACOV GPO)

Chapter Ten

That morning, Natan had been in prison, alone except in his imagination. By evening, he was in Israel, surrounded by thousands of people. All the Jews who had worked for so many years, who had demonstrated and fought and protested, could see that they had accomplished something. Despite all the times they had almost lost hope, they had freed Natan.

Natan made a speech in the stumbling Hebrew that he had never stopped practicing, even in prison. He thanked them for everything they had done. He was only free, he said, "because Jews everywhere in the world understood that the fate of Jews in any country is their fate, too."

But he also told them that the fight was not over.

"On this happiest day of our lives," he said, "I am not going to forget those whom I left in the camps, or those who still continue their struggle for their human rights."

Three months after being released, Natan went to the

Standing Together

United States for ten days to talk to people there about how to continue the struggle.

Avital did not go with him. Now that Natan was home, she was done with public appearances and interviews. (She did not appear in public again until twenty years later, when she spoke at a rally in Jerusalem. Although she had made hundreds of speeches on his behalf, that was the first time Natan ever heard Avital give a speech!)

But luckily for Natan, she had learned a lot during her years of working for his freedom. She had good advice for him.

Soon after being freed, Natan travelled to the United States and met President Ronald Reagan in the Oval Office on October 12, 1986. (White House Photographic Collection)

"Understand," she told him, "our first allies are the students and the housewives. They'll get things started. The leaders will be the last to join.

"But," she finished, "when the leaders finally do join, they'll take all the credit. And then you will know you have won."

During a speech in New York, Natan announced his plan: "What we need now," he said, "is the biggest march in support of Soviet Jews ever. When Gorbachev comes to Washington, D.C. to meet President Reagan, he should see four hundred thousand Jews, to match the four hundred thousand refuseniks still waiting for their visas in the Soviet Union."

Everyone was horrified. The largest rally of Jews in Washington, D.C. before that had been twelve thousand people. There was no way they could get hundreds of thousands to come, in the middle of the winter, with only a few months to prepare!

Leaders of the Jewish community warned him privately: "You're not going to be able to pull this off."

They were wrong. American Jews came to Washington, D.C. that winter. They came in buses, on planes, on trains. So many Jews came from New York City that there were almost no chartered buses left in the city that day. Three huge planes came from Chicago, entirely full of Jews. Overnight buses arrived from Buffalo, Pittsburgh, and Cincinnati. Jews came all the way across

Standing Together

the country, from Texas and California and Florida, and from Toronto, Canada as well. It was a freezing day, but they came anyhow, a sea of people holding up banners, shivering in the cold, and standing together.

Natan sat on the stage with a group of other refuseniks, the Jews with whom he had studied Hebrew in secret and spoken to through toilets in prison cells. They watched the hundreds of thousands of people who had come to support them, and who had—even when they were sitting alone in Soviet prisons—been supporting them all along.

The huge march in support of Soviet Jews that Natan planned took place in Washington, D.C. in December 1987. (Sharansky Family Archive)

As well as making trips abroad, Natan was a public figure in Israel. Here he is with French actor and singer Yves Montand (right) and Prime Minister Shimon Peres (left) in 1986. They are looking at an album of the prime minister's visit to Paris. (Government Photographic Office, Israel)

Natan also met British Prime Minister Margaret Thatcher in 1986. (Government Photographic Office, Israel)

Natan hugging another newly released Soviet prisoner, Ida Nudel. Prime Minister Yitzhak Shamir (left) and Foreign Minister Shimon Peres (right) are with her. (Government Photographic Office, Israel)

In 1996 Natan was Israel's trade minister. Here he is (left) with Israel's fourth president, Professor Ephraim Katzir (centre) and Foreign Minister David Levy (right). (Government Photographic Office, Israel)

From 2001 to 2003, Natan was Israel's minister of construction and housing. (Government Photographic Office, Israel)

Natan was minister of Jerusalem affairs from 2003 to 2005. This photo from 2003 shows him touring Jerusalem's Perimeter Road, together with student leaders. (Government Photographic Office, Israel)

Natan with a thousand Jewish students marching in Jerusalem in 2003. (Government Photographic Office, Israel)

Natan drove a tractor at the Jerusalem Day Parade in 2003. (Government Photographic Office, Israel)

As part of the opening ceremony for the Sakharov Gardens in Jerusalem in 2003, Natan painted the entrance sign. (Government Photographic Office, Israel)

Here Natan is with his bodyguard during a tour of the Gilo neighbourhood of Jerusalem in 2004. (Government Photographic Office, Israel)

Chapter Eleven

In 1991, five and a half years after Natan's release, the Soviet Union broke apart into multiple countries. The government that had kept him in prison for nine years, which had seemed like it would last forever, was no more.

The fall of the Soviet Union shocked everyone—except Natan and his fellow dissidents. They had known all along that the power of freedom would eventually destroy the Soviet Union.

In the ten years that followed Natan's release, over a million Russian Jews emigrated to Israel. Most of them were not activists or refuseniks; they were the silent majority that the refuseniks had always known were there, the ones who were too afraid to say what they really believed.

Natan's mother and brother came to Israel as well. His father, unfortunately, had died of a heart attack while Natan was in prison.

Natan decided to form a new political party to help

Standing Together

Russian immigrants in Israel. His party won many votes and was able to be part of the government. They helped Russian immigrants adjust to life in Israel and become part of Israeli society.

But Natan was never really comfortable with politics. When he was a refusenik, the fight to free him had united different kinds of Jews from all over the world. But as a politician in Israel, he found himself fighting for one group of Jews—those who had voted for him—against other groups who disagreed with him. He felt he was dividing the Jewish people instead of bringing them together.

"It was such a great time when you were in prison," a neighbor told him once. "We were all going to demonstrations, we were all friends. Where did it all go?"

Natan almost apologized for being out of prison! Even though he thought life was much better now ... he understood what his neighbor meant.

Natan was also in disagreement with everyone else in the government about peace with the Palestinians. He believed that the Palestinians should have their own state—but not under a dictator. He thought that the world needed to support those Palestinians who wanted democracy, just as it had supported the dissidents who had fought for democracy in the Soviet Union.

Almost nobody agreed with him. "Your theories are good for the dungeons of the KGB," one prime minister told him, "not the sands of the Middle East."

Standing Together

Natan resigned from the government twice over disagreements about the peace process. Finally, he decided that he'd had enough of politics. When he was invited to join the government again, he declined.

"I spent nine years in prison," he said, "and nine years in politics. That seems like a good balance."

Instead, he asked to be appointed the head of the Jewish Agency.

People were shocked by this request. The Jewish Agency was a very old organization that had once done a great deal to help Jews move to Israel, but now seemed old-fashioned and powerless. Many people argued that it shouldn't exist anymore. But Natan didn't care that the position was seen as a step backward. He believed that as the head of the Jewish Agency, he could return to what he loved to do most: bringing Jews together.

～

No matter how busy he was, Natan went to the airport whenever he could, to watch new immigrants walk onto Israeli soil.

Five years after his arrival in Israel, he got his most exciting opportunity to welcome new immigrants: he helped with the airlift of Ethiopian Jews to Israel. Looking around at the Ethiopian Jews on the plane, he recognized the expressions on their faces. Their

Natan making a speech in 2009 as chairman of the Jewish Agency at a ceremony for new immigrants from the United States. (Government Photographic Office, Israel)

Here Natan is laying a wreath on Holocaust Memorial Day in Yad VaShem in 2011. (Government Photographic Office, Israel)

Even though he stepped away from politics in 1995, Natan was still connected to the leaders. Here he is with Israel's Prime Minister Benjamin Netanyahu on June 18, 2013. (Government Photographic Office, Israel)

Natan giving a speech at the 2015 International Bible Contest. (Government Photographic Office, Israel)

Standing Together

confidence in the future and their lack of fear reminded him of how he had felt on his first flight to Israel.

∽

While he was traveling for the government, Natan had the opportunity to visit his prison. Reporters wondered why he would want to go back to a place that held such painful memories. But for Natan, it was not painful. This was where KGB agents had told him that the refusenik movement was over, that he was completely alone, and that he would never get out alive. Now he stood in that same place, but this time, Avital was

On an official visit to Moscow in 1999, Natan got to see the files prepared for his trial again—fifteen thousand pages in fifty-one volumes. (Sharansky Family Archive)

with him, and he was here as a representative of the government of Israel.

He even went to see his punishment cell. The prison guards first tried to pretend there were no punishment cells anymore, but Natan insisted. "I'll show you where they are," he said. He wanted to show it to Avital.

"Do you recognize this cell?" he asked her. "You were always in here with me."

"I know I was," she replied.

༄

Today Natan and Avital celebrate two seders every year.

One is the Passover seder, during which he, Avital, their two daughters, and their grandchildren recount the story of how the Jews were freed from Egypt.

The other seder is held on the anniversary of the day he was released from Soviet prison. He wears a kippah that his cellmate sewed from the lining of his boots, and tells his children and grandchildren about how he was freed from the Soviet Union.

When the seder is over, Natan and his family dance around the table, singing the same songs he danced to when he first landed on the soil of Israel and rejoined his people.

Afterword

I first heard Natan Sharansky speak in person at a rally at the National Mall in Washington, D.C., on November 14, 2023. It was almost thirty-six years after he had helped lead the rally for Soviet Jews in that same place. He was one of the leaders of this rally, too, and one of the featured speakers.

By that time, over the course of writing this book and preparing it for publication, I had listened to countless recorded interviews with Sharansky and read almost everything he had ever written. Yet on that day in November, as I listened to his words in real time, I found myself inspired all over again:

> *"In the long years of prison, I was told again and again that I was alone.*
> *"But I remembered the faces of Jews who came to Moscow to support us.*
> *"And I knew the KGB was lying."*

Standing Together

> *"A small group of Soviet Jews challenged the most powerful Empire of those days.*
> *"That's why many people thought their struggle, our struggle, is doomed.*
> *"How can a small number bring down an Empire on their own?*
> *"But the fact is that we never thought we were alone."*

As I stood listening, with the U.S. Capitol visible to the right of me and the Washington Monument rising far to my left, the entire space between them filled with people, I thought about the first time hundreds of thousands of Jews had filled this space, rallying for Soviet Jews.

While writing this book, I often wondered what I would have done if I were part of the struggle. Now I asked myself again, as I had been for weeks: Do I have what it takes to live through hard times? Do I have the strength to hold onto hope when everything seems hopeless?

> *"How to keep going?"* Sharansky asked on the stage.
> *"We keep going by doing it together.*
> *"Because we are one Jewish family.*
> *"As long as we all stand together, and fight together, we will win."*

Acknowledgments

My first and deepest gratitude goes to Natan Sharansky and all the other courageous Soviet Jewish dissidents, as well as to those who helped and stood with them.

I am also thankful to the writers, filmmakers, and translators (many of whom are listed in the bibliography) who helped keep their stories from being forgotten.

It's an honor to play a small part in telling that story, and I owe it to those who gave me the opportunity to write and publish this book. A huge thank you to Catriella Freedman, who first suggested that I consider writing this biography; to Rachel Goodman, for her suggestions and support; to Michael Leventhal of Green Bean Books, who acquired and published this book; to Jessica Cuthbert-Smith, for editing; and to Mandy Norman, for the cover.

Thank you to those who helped me research, edit, and revise: Dovid Cypess, Hadassah Cypess, Shoshana Cypess, Tikva Cypess, Shmuel Reuven Gilbert, Stefani

Standing Together

Hoffman, Yakov Koff, Faygie Levy, Allison Marcus, Chaim Yitzi Sternman, and Aviva Werner.

Thank you to Gil Troy for reading an earlier version of this manuscript and providing valuable feedback.

Thank you to the late Vladimir Bukovsky, a Soviet dissident who first coined the explanation of *samizdat* that I quoted on Page 19.

And last but not least, thank you to everyone who has supported me in writing this book—my family, my friends, my community, and my readers.

Timeline

1948: Natan Sharansky is born
1950: Avital Sharansky is born
1953: Joseph Stalin dies
1964: Students' Struggle for Soviet Jewry is founded
1966: Natan Sharansky is accepted into the Moscow Institute of Physics and Technology
1967: The Six-Day War
1968: Andrei Sakharov writes his famous essay
1971: The Thirty-Fives form to protest the imprisonment of a thirty-five-year-old refusenik
1973: Natan applies for an exit visa; Natan and Avital meet; Natan's visa request is refused
1974: Natan and Avital get married, and Avital leaves for Israel
1975: Natan starts working with Andrei Sakharov
1977: Natan is arrested
1978: Natan's trial
1980: Natan is transferred to a labor camp

Standing Together

1982: Natan begins his hunger strike on Yom Kippur
1983: Natan is offered early release if he will request it for medical reasons
1984: Avital meets President Reagan
1985: Reagan and Gorbachev meet in Switzerland
1986: Natan is released
1987: March on Washington for Soviet Jewry
1991: Dissolution of the Soviet Union

Biographies

Leonid Brezhnev

Leonid Brezhnev was the fifth leader of the Soviet Union, and held power for eighteen years, from 1964 until 1982. Brezhnev wanted to be admired and loved like Stalin had been, and tried to use propaganda to convince people that he was an exceptional leader. But among many Soviet citizens he had a reputation for not being very smart, and people often (secretly) told jokes about him.

Jimmy Carter

Jimmy Carter was the president of the United States from 1977 until 1981. He tried to negotiate a treaty with the Soviet Union to reduce the number of nuclear weapons each country produced. However, when the Soviet Union invaded Afghanistan in 1979, President Carter ended the treaty discussions.

Mikhail Gorbachev

Mikhail Gorbachev was the last leader of the Soviet Union, and held power from 1985 until the Soviet Union fell in 1991. He attempted to reform the Soviet Union by changing the way the government ran its economy and by creating a somewhat more free and open society.

Rabbi Shlomo Goren

Rabbi Shlomo Goren was the chief rabbi who, after Natan was arrested, asked Jews worldwide to pray for Soviet Jews. He served as the third chief rabbi of Israel, from 1972 until 1983. Before that, he was the chief rabbi of the Israeli army and created the army's prayer book. After his term as chief rabbi, he established and ran a yeshiva in Jerusalem.

Rav Tzvi Yehuda Kook

Rav Tzvi Yehuda Kook was the rabbi Avital visited after finding out about Natan's arrest. He was the son of Rav Abraham Isaac Kook, who was the first Ashkenazi chief rabbi of pre-state Israel. Both father and son served as the heads of the most prominent religious-Zionist yeshiva in the world, Mercaz HaRav in Jerusalem.

Richard Nixon

Richard Nixon was the president of the United States from 1969 until 1974. One of his goals was to improve the United States' relationships with the two most powerful Communist countries at the time, the Soviet Union and China.

Ronald Reagan
Ronald Reagan was the president of the United States from 1981 until 1989. He was firmly against Communism and once referred to the Soviet Union as "an evil Empire." Later during his presidency, though, he attempted to improve relationships with the Soviet Union. He met with Mikhail Gorbachev, the Soviet leader, to discuss a new treaty to reduce the number of nuclear weapons each country held.

Raiza Palatnik
Raiza Palatnik was a Soviet Jewish librarian who was harassed by the Soviet government after she applied to emigrate to Israel. She was falsely accused of theft, and when her apartment was searched, the KGB found copies of articles about Jewish subjects. She was arrested and sentenced to two years of imprisonment and forced labor, during which she became sick due to the terrible conditions in prison. Her suffering spurred the creation of the "Thirty-Fives," a group of women who campaigned for the freedom of Raiza Palatnik and all other refuseniks. Raiza Palatnik was eventually released from prison and emigrated to Israel.

Standing Together

Andrei Sakharov

Andrei Sakharov was a Soviet physicist who was involved in the development of nuclear weapons for the Soviet Union. He was considered an important scientist and was given privileges by the Soviet government. But he shocked everyone by publishing an essay that criticized aspects of Soviet society and insisted on the importance of freedom of thought. After that, Sakharov was persecuted by the Soviet government. He was awarded the Nobel Peace Prize in 1975 but was not allowed to leave the Soviet Union to accept it.

Joseph Stalin

Joseph Stalin was the second leader of the Soviet Union. He held power for longer than any other leader—for twenty-nine years, from 1924 until 1953. Stalin was an absolute dictator who killed anyone he thought might threaten his power. Under his rule, the Soviet secret police arrested millions of people and used torture to get people to confess to whatever crimes they were accused of, whether true or not.

At the same time, Stalin managed to convince most Soviet citizens that he was a kind-hearted ruler who lovingly took care of his people. Signs declaring, "Thank you, Comrade Stalin, for our happy childhood!" hung in every school. Many people were devastated when he died.

Selected Bibliography

Beckerman, Gal. *When They Come for Us, We'll Be Gone: The Epic Struggle to Save Soviet Jewry*. Mariner Books, 2010.

Bialis, Laura, dir. *Refusenik* (film). The Foundation for Documentary Projects, 2007.

Danziger, Rachel Sharansky. "50 Years Ago, a Failed Hijacking Brought Light into the World", *Times of Israel*, 14 December 2020.

Gilbert, Martin. *Shcharansky: Hero of Our Time*. Viking, 1986.

Nudel, Ida. *A Hand in the Darkness: The Autobiography of a Refusenik*. Translated by Stefani Hoffman. Warner Books, Inc., 1990.

Sharansky, Natan. *Fear No Evil*. Translated by Stefani Hoffman. PublicAffairs, 1998.

Sharansky, Natan, with Ron Dermer. *The Case for Democracy: The Power of Freedom to Overcome Tyranny and Terror*. PublicAffairs, 2004.

Sharansky, Natan, with Shira Wolosky Weiss. *Defending Identity: Its Indispensable Role in Protecting Democracy.* PublicAffairs, 2008.

Sharansky, Natan, with Gil Troy. *Never Alone: Prison, Politics, and My People.* PublicAffairs, 2020.

Shcharansky, Avital, with Ilana Ben-Joseph. *Next Year in Jerusalem.* William Morrow and Co. Inc., 1979.

Weiss, Avi. *Open Up the Iron Doors: Memoirs of a Soviet Jewry Activist.* Toby Press, 2015.